Cel\heartsuit
Seltzer

January 3rd
1983

S0-AUC-545

PARABLES FOR TEACHING

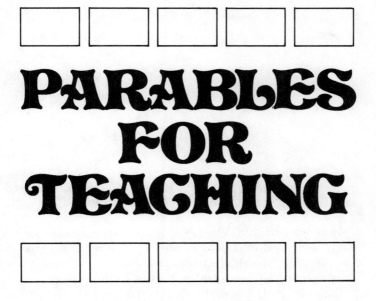

PARABLES FOR TEACHING

Lindsay R. Curtis, M.D.

BOOKCRAFT
Salt Lake City, Utah

Copyright © 1981 by Bookcraft, Inc.

All rights reserved. This book or any part thereof may
not be reproduced in any form whatsoever, whether
by graphic, visual, electronic, filming, microfilming,
tape recording, or any other means, without the prior
written permission of Bookcraft, Inc., except in the
case of brief passages embodied in critical reviews and
articles.

Library of Congress Catalog Card Number: 81-65695
ISBN O-88494-423-9

First Printing, 1981

Lithographed in the United States of America
PUBLISHERS PRESS
Salt Lake City, Utah

Contents

Preface

Frequently I have been asked why I use analogies so often. There are two principal reasons. First, the parables of the New Testament have always had a fastidious fascination for me. The Master Teacher used this method so effectively to teach all classes and cultures.

Second, Nephi, one of my all-time champions, as he read and reread Isaiah from the brass plates, said: "For I did liken all scriptures unto us, that it might be for our profit and learning." (1 Nephi 19:23.) Not only can the scriptures be likened to us, but many of the objects about us, whether simple or complex, can also serve as easy-to-remember parables.

Most of our preaching falls upon unremembering minds, but if we can visualize a simile, a word picture, a parable, we are much more likely to remember it. I hope people won't tire of these homey comparisons to life. They have been and will always be a characteristic of my teaching and writing.

May you find "profit and learning" in these sometimes unscholarly similes.

1
Acoustic Listening

Have you ever stood in a steel-lined room, a boiler factory, or a foundry? Have you ever placed your head in a tank when someone beat on the side?

You are surrounded by sharp overtones and reverberations that could quickly drive you out of your mind. Steel magnifies, mixes up, then throws back every sound that comes to it.

Acoustic tile, on the other hand, absorbs, softens — yes, it even seems to listen intently and compassionately to every sound. When and if it does allow any reverberations, they are mellowed and inoffensive.

Those of us who counsel others must first learn to listen acoustically. We must listen without comment. We must absorb understandingly.

It is so tempting to impulsively offer a quick solution to a problem that has barely iceberged its nose above water. Some people are so flattered by the fact that someone seeks their counsel that they can scarcely wait to give that counsel and thereby demonstrate their wisdom.

Most people who seek counseling have lived with their problem for some time. No doubt they have reviewed it continually in their own minds, and more often than not they have arrived at a pretty sensible solution to their problem. Why, then, do they seek counsel from others?

First, they want to rehearse their problem and solution before someone to see how it sounds "out loud." Second, they want to know if that someone agrees with their already-arrived-at solution.

A sage counselor has learned to listen intently (without interrupting) and acoustically until the individual has presented the entire problem. Then he may say: "No doubt you have been reviewing this problem in your mind for some time. What do *you* think would be the wisest solution to your problem?"

In nearly every case the counselor will find that the individual does indeed have an answer to his problem. He *does* know what he should do about it.

But the counselor's listening to the problem and absorbing it, like acoustic tile, has softened the problem and allowed him to see if the solution *is* sensible. The listener's interest in him may have given him the confidence he needed to handle the problem the way he knows it should be handled anyway.

Before giving counsel (even though it has been asked for), allow the individual an opportunity to present his own solution to the problem. His answer may be better than yours, and he is more likely to follow it if he has *his own* idea.

Like acoustic tile, be absorbent of sound, especially the sound of sorrowing souls. More than anything else they are searching for a compassionate, understanding, listening ear.

2
Are You a Glow Plug?

I bought an automobile with a diesel engine, and thus began an entirely new experience in driving. With diesel comes a masterpiece of precision with a long-lasting engine and with economy in fuel consumption, but also with noise and decreased power.

But there is something else that is interesting about a diesel engine. One does not simply turn the key and start the engine right away. Because the fuel must be ignited under compression at a higher temperature, the engine is equipped with "glow plugs" that must first be given time to glow before they can deliver sufficient spark to ignite the diesel fuel.

If one tries to start the engine before these plugs have had sufficient time to warm up and glow, the engine will not start. To caution against starting too soon, a small light labeled *wait* comes on when the key is first turned to on. This light does not turn off until the allotted time has passed and the plugs are glowing.

For someone not used to waiting in the car for anything, a few seconds seem like hours. For such individuals waiting for the light to go out is an impatient interlude.

But besides patience this "diesel disposition" has taught me a valuable lesson in spirituality. For instance, as I attended church the other day I was impressed with the value of the soft, serene prelude music. It permitted time for pondering, for putting thoughts in tune with the reverent feeling of the sacrament service. It gave my soul an opportunity to turn on and tune into the spirit of the sermon. A burning, a glowing feeling, came within my heart as the music continued.

Have you ever called your family together for family home evening and noticed the sign *wait* light up in their minds? Have you ever found it difficult to get into the mood for proper prayer or for dedicated devotion because of the *wait* signal?

Sometimes a soft word, a kind sentence of appreciation, a meaningful nod of the head, even the wink of an eye, will start the plugs glowing.

Attitudes in families and individuals can be ignited by glow plugs that warm the heart and quicken the spirit. Let us look for those whose spirits are low, whose hearts are heavy, and light the glow plugs that fire up *their* spiritual engines.

3
As the Tree Is Notched

The bark beetles had been busy destroying many of the proud, well-proportioned pines surrounding our cabin, trees that had long befriended us by shading us from the sun and warding off the wind. Burrowing through the bark, these pesky bugs sapped the strength of these stalwart sons of the forest.

The once-green needles were now brown and brittle. The trunks of some of these magnificent monarchs were parched, bone-dry, and ready to pop with the next wind. Because of their proximity to the cabin, they posed a serious problem.

If they fell in the direction of the cabin, they would quickly crush it to the ground like a cardboard box. It was urgent that they be removed. But how to do it and not endanger the cabin was the question.

I bought a chain saw and carefully read the instructions. If I cut a notch on the side of the tree opposing the cabin, then sawed at a lower level on the side toward the cabin, the tree should fall in the direction of the notch and away from the cabin. It seemed simple and logical. Just follow the directions. Even the illustrations made it look elementary.

Carefully I primed the motor and pulled on the cord, and to my delight the chain saw whizzed after the second pull. Taking due aim with my general sense of where the tree should fall, I began to make the notch. After some initial difficulty, the wedge of wood finally fell from the notch.

Next I began to saw on the opposite side at a lower level. Soon the tree would tumble exactly where I wanted it — or so I thought. I was partially right. It did fall, not falteringly but with a flourish. But not where I thought it would.

In what could have been a terrible tragedy the tree barely missed the cabin, crashing like thunder to the ground only a few feet from total calamity. I had nearly caused the very disaster I had hoped to avoid!

The deed was done, and the shock had partially subsided. But my heart was still pounding heavily as I pondered the possible. What could have happened and nearly did happen? Why didn't the tree fall where I thought it would? where I had intended it to fall? where I had planned for it to fall? the way I thought I had notched?

After the fact I studied the situation more closely. Carefully I now eyed the angles. Where had I miscalculated? What had gone wrong? There were several reasons — the wind, the leaning of the tree. All of these probably played a role.

But when it came right down to the deciding factor, I had really misfigured the angle of the notch. Too casually I had sighted the situation. Too carelessly I had handled the saw as it bit into the trunk of the tree. Actually the tree had fallen exactly as I had notched it. Unwittingly I had planned for it to fall just where it fell.

There is a lesson to be learned in all of this.

The Lord has given us our free agency. He gives each of us a body, a mind, and a place on earth to develop these. On this body and mind He hangs a sign that says: "Will build to suit tenant." Then He leaves it up to us as to how and what we want Him to help us build for the tenant — ourselves.

We sight the notches. We determine where the tree will fall. We handle the saw. He is only the consultant engineer. He lets us make the decisions. He will nod His head to let us know if we have made the correct decisions if we ask Him. But usually He doesn't interfere. The rules are written. They are unmistakable and they are unalterable.

As the tree is notched, so will it fall. And I'm glad it's that way, but the responsibility is completely our own.

4
The Beacon
That Wouldn't Beckon

It was just outside Atlanta, Georgia, that we saw Stone Mountain. A Salt Lake Tabernacle-shaped dome of solid granite about a mile in diameter and over eight hundred feet high. Because this is the largest block of solid granite in the world, it is only natural that it should become the sight of the largest carved monument in the world.

The South is proud of its three heroes (Confederate President Jefferson Davis, General Robert E. Lee, and General Stonewall Jackson) whose images ride forever (on horses) on the side of this majestic mountain. This impressive panorama stands over 80 feet tall and 180 feet wide.

The history of this monument, which took fifty-five years and two sculptors to complete, is punctuated by disappointments, frustrations, long layoffs, and finally tremendous triumph. Undoubtedly it is one of the wonders of the world that will endure for thousands of years.

But one of the most intriguing true stories has to do with a safety light that was to be built on top of Stone Mountain. At a time when night-flying instruments were few and extremely crude, the mail was carried in little single-seated biplanes that attempted to dispense overnight service between Atlanta and New York.

Because Stone Mountain lay directly in the path of flight, the pilot insisted that a safety light be built atop the dome. A contractor was commissioned and the laborious task of toting steel poles and wire up the steep trail began.

Tower and beacon were completed and nothing more was said until one dark night when pilot Johnny Kytle's plane smashed into Stone Mountain, spreading bags of mail all over its steep slope. Where was the safety light? Why couldn't the pilot see it?

Investigation proved embarrassing, for it showed that *there was no light.*

The contractor was summoned to account for the lack of light in the tower. Producing his work sheet, the foreman checked off each item — the poles, bolts and braces, the insulators, the wire, the docket, and, the final item, he had turned on the electricity.

But nowhere in the contract had it called for a light bulb, so he hadn't supplied it. All he had to do was to screw one bulb into the socket. This, however, he felt was not his responsibility. And so the lack of a bulb costing only a few cents nearly cost the life of a pilot.

Does this remind you of a scripture? "It is not meet that I should command in all things; for he that is compelled in all things, the same is a slothful and not a wise servant.... men should ... do many things of their own free will." (D&C 58:26, 27.)

Is it possible that our performance on this earth will be measured by how far we have gone in the second mile, the mile we were not required to travel?

Let's be sure that the light in our beacon is turned on. A beckoning beacon could save some eternal lives.

5
Be Careful of Candy Coating

One of the most common causes of death in children is by poisoning. And the most common cause of this poisoning is by taking candy-coated pills. One simple answer given by some who wish to prevent these tragic deaths is to make certain that there is no candy coating on medical pills.

But children take other poisons too, mostly out of curiosity. Very young children in particular tend to taste everything. If you have ever watched them, you'll see that most things they can move (and some they can't) go directly into their mouths. Even without the candy coating, children will still experiment with poisons. While we agree that candy coatings are undesirable as far as children are concerned, adults might also have a difficult time swallowing their medicine without that coating.

Another sensible solution is that we keep pills out of the reach of children. Most of us try to do that. But occasionally children have a way of reaching even those things that supposedly are impossible to reach.

These two solutions are similar to those suggested to prevent children from drowning. We can build fences around pools and erect high gates, but the best preventive of tragic drownings is to teach children at an early age to swim.

Likewise, the best method to prevent poisoning is to teach children at an early age to ask their parents first before they put *anything* into their mouths. Studies have shown that children *can* be taught the importance of this rule and that they can be taught it at an early age when they are most likely to get into poisons. It takes effort, it takes time, it takes patience; but it can be done.

Just as deadly and perhaps of more importance in the eternal nature of things is the great array of spiritual poisons which people ingest and from which many of them die spiritually. Even in our Church the mortality rate is frighteningly high. Spiritual mortality in the world at large has reached astronomical figures.

Most of us are familiar with some of the common physical poisons: aspirin, tranquilizers, sleeping pills. Also such caustics as lye, cleaning fluids and powders, insect poisons are definite health hazards.

The constant diet of peer pressure to ignore the standards which the Lord has revealed to us through our prophet is one that slowly but definitely poisons the soul. Drugs at school, cigarettes for sociability, and alcohol frequently from parents' own alcoves are all contributing to the steady poisoning of our children.

If pornography does not come from peers it is in ample supply from unconscionable adults. Who publishes the pornographic portrayals in magazines and books? Not the children, but the adults. Television wantonly trudges right into our living room with its pernicious plots of infidelity and premarital sex, laughing at morality and calling chastity old-fashioned.

These poisons are not only candy coated, but if they are not intercepted and identified for what they really are, they may become so palatable that children will seek them as a steady diet.

Yes, physical poisoning among children is a serious problem, but the poisoning of their minds may be an even greater threat and one which will threaten their eternal life.

And our best preventive is to teach them not to put anything into their minds until they have made certain that it is not a poison.

6
Bloodletting or Transfusion

There was a time when medicine's two principal remedies were purgatives and bloodletting. Small wonder that the mortality rate was high and public confidence was low.

Undoubtedly many suffering souls were ushered into the next world prematurely by these two ill-advised procedures. Consider an individual afflicted with an acute appendix. The last thing such a patient should have would be a purgative.

Think of someone struggling with every ounce of available effort and resistance against an infection. The worst thing that could happen to such an individual would be a further lowering of his resistance against that infection by a loss of some of his disease-fighting blood. In fact, his blood might already be low (anemia) as a result of the infection. The treatment would be to give him a transfusion rather than a bloodletting.

We can't criticize the past or its people because we don't know all of the circumstances surrounding their situation. But we might apply some of these lessons of the past to the present.

For instance, when an individual is suffering from a chronic erosion of his self-esteem, when his self-image is at an all-time low, the last thing he needs is further criticizing, moralizing, or preaching. This is tantamount to bloodletting in an anemic individual. What he really needs is a transfusion of sincere praise for performance, recognition for reliability, appreciation for initiative, or commendation for courage.

Someone who is inactive in the Church doesn't need castigation for noncompliance with the commandments. He is already very much aware of his follies and failures. What he really needs is a spiritual transfusion, something that touches his soul, gives him courage, and then moves him to make whatever change is necessary in himself and his life.

Listen to one of the great spiritual transfusions given by the Savior Himself, to the Nephites during His appearance on this American continent: "And...while they were thus conversing one with another, they heard a voice as if it came out of heaven; and they cast their eyes round about, for they understood not the voice which they heard; and it was not a harsh voice, neither was it a loud voice; nevertheless, and notwithstanding it being a small voice it did pierce them that did hear to the center, insomuch that there was no part of their frame that it did not cause to quake; yea, it did pierce them to the very soul, and did cause their hearts to burn." (3 Nephi 11:3.)

When we speak to our fellow men and women with love in our hearts, in kindness and compassion, when we understand them and their particular problems, then we can converse with them from heart to heart. The result will be a spiritual transfusion to their soul as it causes their "hearts to burn." And it will help them to recover from their spiritual illness.

Before we cajole, call to repentance, criticize, or

moralize our neighbor, let us ponder to be sure we give him not a spiritual bloodletting but a spiritual transfusion.

7
Constriction of the Heart

Only a few times in my medical career have I seen the condition in the living, but I can well remember the first time I saw a case at the autopsy table. It was called chronic constrictive pericarditis. This really doesn't mean much to a lay person, but let me describe it to you.

A normal heart is encased in a well-lubricated sac called the pericardium. This sac has several functions, one of the most important of which is to allow the heart to expand and contract freely as it pumps blood throughout the body. Another function is to protect it from irritation on the outside, to lubricate the outside of the heart muscle (the heart is really a large bundle of hard-working muscle fibers) so that its movement will not be hindered by friction. This sac also gives a general extra covering to the heart, similar to a layer of plastic wrap but it permits sliding and slipping in any direction to accommodate each contraction.

But occasionally the sac itself becomes irritated and infected. When this happens, the inflammation causes a thickening of the sac's layers, eventually permitting the sac to become glued to the heart muscle itself. The result is a thick, scarred, unwieldy layer of inelastic fibrous tissue that does just the opposite to what it was originally intended to do. Instead of aiding, it restricts the movement of the heart.

Instead of allowing the heart to expand freely, progression of the disease process begins to contract and constrict the heart. This constrictive narrowing of this leathery encasement works like a vise as it causes irregularity of the beat, ineffectiveness of the stroke of the heart, and ultimately heart failure. The heart is actually squeezed to a smaller size and is therefore less able to do its job of pumping blood to the body.

When constrictive pericarditis persists, it demands dramatic treatment, which consists of cutting this heavy, unwieldy layer away from the heart. Such surgery once more gives the heart its freedom to expand and contract as necessary to meet the needs of the body.

Sometimes a similar process takes place spiritually. When we become insensitive to the needs of others, when we are so taken up by the things of the world that we forget the Lord and His needy children, we become victims of chronic constrictive spiritual pericarditis. We wrap a tight, inflexible layer of selfishness around our heart that restricts it from caring about others who are in need. If not treated early and effectively, this process of tightening around the heart constricts more and more until the heart becomes totally nonfunctioning as far as spiritual things are concerned. We forget all about the teachings of Jesus Christ and His counsel that we are our brother's keeper. Just as a constricted heart loses its resiliency, so a spiritually impaired heart becomes incapable of compassion and concern.

Fortunately there is an excellent cure for this condition. The risk is low, the mortality is nil, and the prognosis is exceptionally optimistic. The treatment is found in this statement from the Savior: "He that loseth his life for my sake shall find it." (Matthew 10:39.)

Though medically speaking the disease is rare, it may be one of the commonest of our remediable spiritual diseases. Let's make sure if we have even the beginning signs of it that we start the treatment right away.

If we lose ourselves in looking out for others, we shall surely find the abundant and the gratifying life for ourselves.

8
Deep Roots Steady Against a Storm

While trail riding one day I saw something interesting. A tall, sturdy, still-green, well-proportioned pine tree had been blown over by the wind. There was no evidence of lightning having struck it. (Lightning is a common cause of destruction, as it splits these giant trees and makes them vulnerable to the wind.)

The bark beetles hadn't touched its trunk nor browned its branches as they had done to many other trees in the area. Why, I wondered, had this majestic model of nature suddenly succumbed to the wind? Its robust roots laced an area at least thirty feet in diameter. Surely this spread should give the tree a wide base of stability.

But intent inspection eventually solved the mystery. Directly under the area formerly covered by its roots there flowed water from a tiny spring. Here the seed for this pine tree had found an easy source of water and had quickly taken root and begun to grow.

With abundant water within easy reach, rapid growth was inevitable for this giant of the forest as it outstripped its siblings in both height and girth. Not dependent upon direct rainfall, this tree knew neither drought nor dry season.

With water so readily available near the surface, this

tree had never had to sink its roots deep into the ground. Although its roots spread over a wide base, they had never anchored themselves deep into the ground like the trees which had to struggle and search over and around rocks, deep into the soil, to find moisture.

When an extra strong wind came along and blew against its succulent branches, the tree toppled over like a fragile lamp with an all-too-light base. It had nothing to anchor it against outside forces. By contrast, its hardy neighbors' roots were securely wrapped around rocks that steadied them against any storm.

We should sink our roots deep into the truths of the gospel of Jesus Christ. Only then will our testimonies stay by us through any trials and troubles that come our way.

9
Does Your Spiritual
Air Filter Need Cleaning?

Except for a few puffs of cotton clouds strategically placed here and there, the sky was an uninterrupted background of blue. The weather was warm enough for comfort, yet cool enough to be invigorating. The scintillating scent of pine needles outperfumed any other aromas of nature on this occasion.

Having planned this trail ride for several weeks, our anticipation of it probably exceeded the actual experience. Each of us came equipped with a trail bike capable of challenging any crest.

Just as we had hoped, the experience thrilled and filled, exhilarated and excited when we drank in the skyline panorama of green, yellow, and red from autumn in the Rockies. Just when this serenity seemed at its climax, just when this thrill was etching itself into our never-to-be-forgotten emotional diaries, it happened.

The motorbike coughed, sputtered, and refused to perform. Only after considerable adjusting, urging, encouraging, cajoling, and reprimanding did the bike barely carry me to the conclusion of our journey. What possibly could have gone wrong with my "friend of the hills" that had always been so reliable? Why, just when its performance was so vital, did it fail me?

It was not until we had returned home and I had pieced together the previous weeks of use that a possible cause was suggested. Could it have been the clouds of dust from a parched earth on that trail ride that had choked me so much that I had to tie a bandanna over my nose and mouth in order to breathe? Slowly it became clear. I had coughed and choked, but what about the motorbike whose impeccable performance I had always taken for granted?

True, before we left I had bathed the outside of the bike until it sparkled for the upcoming ride. But what about *its* "lungs"? I had neglected to clean them. In a matter of moments I loosened a few screws and removed the air filter.

On a motorbike, the air must filter through a sponge lightly soaked in oil in order to remove any dust particles before it can enter the carburetor. Such a cleansing helps to insure superior performance.

To my embarrassment the filter (the engine's "lungs") was shamefully choked with the dust from the previous ride. Yes, I had swabbed the bike's exterior for appearance sake, but totally neglected the interior.

My own lungs I had shielded from the destructive dust with a bandanna, which could be later laundered. But the motorbike still struggled to breathe through a dirt-fogged filter, coughing and gasping gulps of air to supply a craving carburetor.

This otherwise dependable device was not broken. But when the grime became too gross to handle, the filter faltered and finally gave up. After a thorough cleansing of the air filter, the motorbike once more performed flawlessly.

Occasionally the same process occurs in our minds. Sometimes we are exposed to unseemly situations.

Our minds, our thought processes, become choked with pornography, baseness, crassness, and crudeness that constantly adorns our almost incredible contemporary culture.

Our consciences may become cluttered with unrepented sins, even minor ones as fine as dust. Sometimes our spiritual channels become choked with the unspiritual, the mundane, and materialistic.

Introspection, insight, pondering, reevaluation of our responsibilities, and reprogramming of our priorities are important. But true repentance is required to clean our spiritual air filters. Only through an undefiled air cleaner can our spirituality take a fresh, deep breath of invigoratingly pure air and feel the exhilaration of the completely redeemed.

Everyone needs an occasional spiritual tune-up to get rid of the grime, grit, and carbon from his mind. While you're at it, check on your spiritual air cleaner to make sure your "skyline ride" back to your Father in Heaven is all it can and should be.

10
Even Snowshoes Can Slip

Did you know that snowshoes were invented by North American Indians? Originally made of webs of rawhide stretched over a willow frame, they transported Indians and trappers over the snow at an amazing walking rate of five miles per hour. Experts could travel at a dogtrot as fast as ten miles an hour.

But have *you* ever tried to travel on these cumbersome, clumsy, and inconvenient clods? Perhaps they are difficult only for the less dexterous like myself.

I have learned one thing from snowshoes. It is tough to attack a hardpacked, heavily crusted hill on these tenuous "tennis rackets." And I discovered that even snowshoes will slip if the slope is steep enough and if the crust of snow is hard or icy. Ideally the crust of snow needs just a little melting, a "trifle of tempering" to allow the snowshoes to stick.

Have you ever encountered people like this? Have you seen souls so stiff, hearts so hardened, that they wouldn't permit anyone to penetrate their outer shells?

I know a man like this. For years he was the man nobody knew or wanted to know. It has taken time. Age has had to mellow his manner, and time has had to tenderize his outer crust of defensive pride.

But when his armor plate was finally pierced, when he softened sufficiently to allow others to love him, a marvelous and merciful man emerged. Inside he had been miserable and lonely. Here was a man who was hungry for the affection and friendship of others, but too proud to proffer his innermost feelings to them. Here was a gentleman who found it difficult to make the first gesture.

No snowshoe of kindness could scale this outer crust until he permitted it to soften a little. Too often pride prevents us from partaking of many pleasures of life.

Most of the time we *want* to be friendly and gracious. Most of us hunger for the love of others. But too often we have been scalded by a scolding, offended by some person's fumbling refutation, burned by some bumbling blunderhead, or ridiculed by a ridiculous remark. Our feelings are fettered, and we place a shell around ourselves that grows thicker and touchier with the passing of time.

It is only natural to erect a protective shell about ourselves to shield us from such an injury. Only when we soften this shell can others once more bestow their gestures of love.

Snowshoes *can* slip and all efforts to fellowship *can* fail if we don't soften our outer shells and go our half of the way.

11
The Gentle Letdown

It was a simple thing. Ordinarily I would have ignored it. But always looking for lessons in life, I found one here.

There was a disquieting "quapp-quapp" under the car, probably nothing important. But then we would be leaving for a long trip in the next few days — better get it checked.

My friend at the garage noticed that the work area into which I had pulled the car had a hoist, and my car seemed to be already well placed over it. With no alteration of the car's position he could raise it in the air to take a look.

"This will take only a moment, stay where you are," he said. "Don't even bother to get out of your car."

The hoist raised the car and myself about six feet in the air, sufficient to give the mechanic a good glance at the underpinnings of the car. A small branch caught in the frame and rubbing on a wheel was readily removed. Then by a flick of his wrist the hydraulic hoist let us down.

As I said, it was a small thing. But I couldn't help but notice how gently the hoist let us descend — no bump, no jerk, no sudden jar as we settled down on the concrete floor.

Yes, a simple thing, but I was reminded of several times in my life when I had been let down, when my friends had been let down, when even those who weren't close friends had been let down, and not very gently. And I was not without blame myself.

There was the time, for instance, when I had brusquely told a patient that her labor would be long and hard, without taking the time to tell her why, and assuring her that all would be well and that I would be standing by to help and to relieve her. I had a lot to learn about tenderness and compassion. I could have eased her letdown so that it would have been gentle and tolerable.

I recall when a timid young teenager practiced long and with great sacrifice to become the greatest cheerleader the school had ever had. She dedicated herself totally to the task. She was turned down not because of lack of skill but because she was too tall — and with no praise for her performance or effort — an abruptly cruel and unnecessary letdown, devoid of the tender explanation that could have softened the fall and cushioned the collapse that followed.

How often are hardworking people in the Church released from positions without the brief expression of praise for a job well done and for effort expended far beyond what had been asked of them?

There is no one who has not experienced a letdown in his or her life. Some have been gentle, some have not. But there are two words that usually help to soften the fall: "I understand."

Let's remember the humble, unheralded hydraulic hoist and recall the soft touch it tenders to those it lets down. When the task becomes ours, let's pattern our performance after it.

12
Gold Depends Upon Where You Look

Most of the trees had lost their leaves. Only an occasional cluster of red leaves clung to an oak here and there. Yellow aspen leaves polka-dotted every path. In the crisp wind was a definite wisp of winter. It would probably be our final foray into the forests before snow spread its sheets over the furniture and pulled the shades until next spring.

Three generations of us, from grandson to grandfather all with the same name, were off to follow a most familiar trail in the mountains. But this day was to be different. For the first time we would cover the same paths with a metal detector. For the first time we would see what lay *under* this ground we had grown to love and had scrutinized (or so we thought) so carefully on so many occasions.

As the detector deliberately scanned the dirt, our first beep bounced back before we had proceeded more than a few paces. Quickly we dug into the ground to see what treasure lay trapped and awaiting us. Sure enough — our first prize. A tarnished, scarcely recognizable penny!

On we went, finding everything from gum-wrapper foil of yesteryear to a bright gold earring. Even decades-old square nails were brought to the surface as booty.

Our ultimate goal was a splendid streambed that held particular fascination for us because three old mines from a century ago had emptied their tailings into this stream. Naturally we amateurs had notions of finding nuggets all over the place.

"If we really want to look for nuggets big enough to detonate the detector, we should look in the center of the bottom of the streambed," my son said.

"Why is that?" I asked.

"Because gold is heavy. It never follows slow-moving water. You will always find it in the center of the stream where its weight has quickly carried it to the bottom."

Gold is certainly not like driftwood that floats and is carried here and there, wherever the water or the wind may take it. Pure gold is heavy. It is not easily diverted in every direction and is moved only by a swift current. Because of its weight, gold is not easily swayed from its path. It seeks the straight path and the deepest water.

We can learn some lessons from gold. The Lord needs souls who are stable, immovable in their aims; souls whose anchors are solid; souls who desire to serve him without wavering.

Anyone can drift with the current, move with the mob, cringe when faced with criticism, or seek popularity with peers. The Lord needs men with relentless resolve, men who have the stability of gold. He needs those who, like gold, follow the straight and narrow way.

You'll find gold and good men and women in the middle of the straight and narrow streams.

13
Hardening of the Heart

Most people are familiar with the term arteriosclerosis or hardening of the arteries. The term *sclerosis* comes from the Greek language and means hardening, most often due to previous inflammation or irritation.

Many organs are subject to sclerosis, including the spinal cord, the brain, the kidneys, and various glands — all with the same deteriorating effect.

But I should like to mention a new type of sclerosis that is not found in medical journals. I doubt if this disease would be acknowledged by the medical profession. I shall call it *cardio*sclerosis, and the ill effects of this disease are neither medical nor physical. Yet these effects may be more serious, even fatal, to the individual.

Cardiosclerosis, as I have named it, means hardening of the heart. It may be found in those who lose their compassion; their understanding of others; their awareness of the suffering, the sorrowing, the lonely, the troubled, the forsaken. It is a disease that turns one's thoughts constantly inward so that a person thinks only of himself and his own needs.

Although others may suffer as a result of an individual's hardheartedness, it is really the person with the disease who ultimately aches most. Soon he is friendless, forlorn; his efforts unfruitful; his life futile.

Many years ago I knew a man whose only admitted goal in life was to accumulate wealth. To him money not only talked, but it monopolized his entire conversation and ultimately his entire life.

Recently he died, having reached his goal, wealthy beyond description. I have wondered how he must have felt when he discovered that he couldn't take any of this wealth with him.

It will be interesting for him to check his ledgers at the judgment seat to see in which color ink, red or black, the important things of life are recorded. He may also be surprised to find cardiosclerosis recorded on his death certificate as the cause of his spiritual demise.

Some cases of medical sclerosis can be prevented, others cannot. Many of these cases are inherited and, so far at least, we know neither how to prevent nor to cure them.

Cardiosclerosis on the other hand, is not inherited. It is a result of careful planning — in the wrong direction. It definitely can be prevented, and in most instances it can be successfully treated if the individual really wants to work at it.

Christ found many instances of this disease in His time and often called it by other names, such as scribes, Pharisees, hypocrites. He also gave various cures for the disease according to the cause. All of them worked when assiduously applied.

"Labour not for the meat which perisheth, but for that meat which endureth unto everlasting life." (John 6:27.)

"Love your enemies, bless them that curse you, do

good to them that hate you, and pray for them which despitefully use you, and persecute you." (Matthew 5:44.)

"Lay not up for yourselves treasures upon earth, where moth and rust doth corrupt, and where thieves break through and steal:

"But lay up for yourselves treasures in heaven, where neither moth nor rust doth corrupt, and where thieves do not break through nor steal:

"For where your treasure is, there will your heart be also." (Matthew 6:19-21.)

A healthy heart, spiritually speaking, perceives a neighbor's needs before they are spoken, sees suffering without having to be shown, and senses unsounded sorrows. A healthy heart responds to the sinner without reproach, goes the second mile without soliciting.

Not only are these the signs of a healthy heart, but they are also the means of preventing spiritual cardiosclerosis. Let's strive for a healthy heart, the kind that leads to eternal longevity.

14
How Much Is
Two Plus Two?

The account in the newspaper was tragic. A nineteen-year-old mountain climber had fallen to his death.

Let's review the facts. Mountain climbing, contrary to many opinions, is safe when undertaken by those who are skilled at it and when those involved obey strictly all of the rules of that challenging sport. It is not a sport for anyone who is careless or cuts corners. It is not for anyone who rationalizes precautions, or for anyone who is less than meticulous about equipment.

Investigation of the tragedy revealed that this youth had used hemp instead of nylon rope. He had not tied the approved safety knots. His anchor was a rock too small. His rope had been tied on the rock in such a fashion that it would saw through. On and on the problems were revealed.

Apparently the young man had hoped that two plus two somehow would not equal four. Using proper procedures, following safety precautions, he would not have had an accident. He would be alive today.

I recall digging a foundation for a cabin that involved removing certain trees. Other trees we figured could be left without impairing their growth. One tree was questionable. If we extended the foundation as far as it really should go, it would jeopardize the roots of this tree and it would die.

We decided to take a chance and leave this majestic tree. Having impaired its source of sustenance, we really had doomed the tree for death. Now it is not only unsightly, but it definitely poses a hazard to the cabin and must be removed.

How often we do this same thing with our own lives! We cut away our spiritual roots hazardously close, weakening and challenging the existence of our spirituality, and then wonder why our testimonies die. How often people die spiritually early in life because they do not follow the rules our Father in Heaven has given us!

How many people have failed to follow the precautions Jesus pointed out to us and then wonder why their families have fallen apart or their relationships have deteriorated? "Seek ye first the kingdom of God, and his righteousness; and all these things shall be added unto you." (Matthew 6:33.)

The Lord put it in another way through the Prophet Joseph Smith: "There is a law irrevocably decreed in heaven before the foundations of this world, upon which all blessings are predicated — And when we obtain any blessing from God, it is by obedience to that law upon which it is predicated." (D&C 130:20-21.)

Yes, two plus two equals four, whether dealing with arithmetic, safety, or souls.

15
How Much Poison
Can You Tolerate?

From a very dear friend of mine I have learned much. This friend's kidneys have failed, and he is now completely dependent upon a dialysis machine. Three times a week he must make this his first priority.

Dialysis has become a household word in the last few years as more and more people find their precarious lives extended by this marvelous method of removing the poisons from the body, poisons that healthy kidneys easily eliminate.

Regardless of the assignment, this courageous and uncomplaining man performs his job most effectively. But he always keeps in mind that he must meet a deadline with his dialysis center.

Instead of giving up, this friend of mine carries on a very demanding job, one that carries him through several states on an extremely tight schedule. Always he must plan ahead very carefully so that he can reach a dialysis center every other day. If he were to neglect this priority just once he would be in serious trouble. More than a day or two delay would place his life in jeopardy.

Poisons in the blood can be tolerated effectively by the body up to a certain level. When they exceed this limit, organs begin to deteriorate, vital functions fail, and death quickly ensues.

But isn't this also true as far as poisoning the mind is concerned? There is a certain amount of poison, filth, and trash in the world to which we are exposed whether we want to be or not. Newspaper ads, movie marquees, television shorts — even casual remarks by those with whom we associate — contribute involuntary, unsolicited, and unwanted filth.

But the mind can tolerate only so much poison without a deleterious effect. Periodically we must subject our mind to a cleansing dialysis that will rid it of these unsavory thoughts, images, and subjects.

Attendance at church, participation in spiritual and uplifting projects, scripture reading, attendance at the temple, observance of the Sabbath — all of these serve as a spiritual dialysis to rid our minds of unwanted and troublesome thoughts.

To safeguard our spiritual health we must make such periodic dialysis a prime priority. To each individual it is left to set up his own schedule for this cleansing process.

We must remember that, just as with someone whose kidneys have failed and whose body can tolerate no more poison without serious damage, we must monitor the level of filth that our minds can tolerate.

A person with impaired kidneys will avoid certain foods in order to keep the level of toxins as low as possible. Likewise, we should be careful of those things to which we subject our minds.

Foreseeing the day when so much corruption and pornography would exist all around us, the Lord counseled: "And that thou mayest more fully keep thyself *unspotted* from the world, thou shalt go to the house of prayer and offer up thy sacraments upon my holy day." (D&C 59:9. Italics added.)

Seems like excellent spiritual dialysis, doesn't it?

16
How to Lighten the Load

It was a fun-filled family project at the Cabin in the Pines. We would dam the stream and make an old-fashioned swimming hole. Not only would we be able to swim and splash, but also to float and flail the stream on inner tubes and rough-hewn rafts, and to enjoy a dozen other water sports.

"Come over here a minute, Dad," my son beckoned. "I want to teach you a lesson." He was supervising the project.

"You'll notice some whopping huge rocks here in the stream that no one can or should lift." Arching their brown backs out of the water like a herd of hippopotami, these mammoth monsters defiantly challenged us to change the course of the stream over which they had exercised sovereign domain for so many centuries. "But they will have to be moved," my son continued. "And I want to show you how it can be done."

It was true, the stones were so heavy that no ordinary man could heft them. In my mind I couldn't see how he could possibly solve this one with muscle power.

"If we take brush," he continued, "small logs, and the smaller stones, and build a small dam first, the water will gradually become deeper. When the level of water rises *above* these heavy rocks, then the water itself will help us accomplish our task of moving them. We'll leave them where they are until we develop some depth to the dam." My son had my complete cooperation, for I wasn't about to strain my back on such big boulders.

He was right. Slowly the water rose above these pompous patriarchs of the stream. But none of these brawny boulders was touched by us until the water was deep enough to cover them completely with some to spare. But once they were covered, it amazed me how even I could move many of them through the water to clear the streambed and to take their place in the dam.

When a boulder is under water, it displaces its own volume in water, hence it also displaces the weight of that amount of water. In other words, the boulder now weighs its normal weight *less* the weight of the water it has displaced. But the water must have sufficient depth to cover the rocks.

The same thing happens in the gospel of Jesus Christ. If we have sufficient depth in the gospel, if we have a deep and abiding faith in Christ, it can help us move mountains. With the help from such a testimony we can withstand spiritually stormy weather and overcome massive obstacles with which we never could hope to cope without such help.

The Savior said: "Come unto me, all ye that labour and are heavy laden, and I will give you rest [help].

"Take my yoke upon you, and learn of me; for I am meek and lowly in heart: and ye shall find rest unto your souls.

"For my yoke is easy, and my burden is light." (Matthew 11:28-30.)

If we first develop sufficient depth in the gospel of

Jesus Christ, this will help us lighten our load, regardless of the size of the obstacles.

17
How Will Your Obituary Read?

This particular obituary rated a special editorial. The man's death did not go unnoticed, definitely not!

"Mr. Blank is dead at sixty-five of congestive heart failure. He died where he belonged — in the prisoners' section of the County Hospital.

"It is customary to speak nothing but good of the dead, but we are forced to make an exception in this case. There is simply nothing good that can be said of him.

"He was a swindler, who, until the law caught up with him, mulcted thousands by selling them worthless desert land. He made our state notorious as the 'land fraud capital of the nation.'

"The state has yet to live down the reputation he gave it. We shed no tears for him. He was a scoundrel, pure and simple."

As I read this obituary, one thought consumed my mind. How must his wife and children feel about such a legacy? How can they ever hold their heads high as long as they bear his name?

Whether he left them money is really not important. What he did leave them — his name — they not only do not want, but without legal procedures they will never be able to rid themselves of it.

Recently I traced the history of a family that originally came into the Church with enormous sacrifice. In
the early days of the Church they were spiritual giants
and would gladly have sacrificed their lives for the
cause if it had been necessary. Their names will be
remembered as having tendered their all for the build-
ing up of our Church. Frequently at the peril of their
lives they stood up for that which they knew was right.

One of their number was eventually called to one of
the highest positions in the Church and served nobly.
All his life wherever his name was heard it provoked
reverence and gratitude in the hearts of faithful
Latter-day Saints.

For little-understood reasons the next generation
was not quite so dedicated. Although they never dis-
claimed their relationship to the Church, they did
little, if anything, for the Church. When persecution
of the Church was evident, they were not.

Recently I talked to the present generation of this
once-stalwart family. Totally disavowing any relationship whatsoever with God's restored Church, he
said that one church seemed to him just as good as the
other. He was quick to point out that the restored
Church had many faults in it, and especially in its
members and leaders.

His children have not been baptized into the Church
and probably never will be if he has anything to do with
it, he assured me.

What has happened to the spirit of conversion that
so moved the forefathers of this family? What happened to the legacy for which they were willing to give
their lives?

As far as the Lord's restored Church is concerned,
this man's name and the names of his children will not
be upon the records. There will be no legacy. Is it

possible that when these descendants realize how their birthright was sold for a mess of pottage that they will feel as the aforementioned state felt about their citizen who had just died?

Question for those who are not members of the Church: If you could know that we had the most valuable thing that you could possibly have on earth, would you be interested in knowing about it? Let's take this a little farther. If you could know with all your heart that this gospel of Jesus Christ is the most valuable possession you have right now, would you take better care not to lose it?

The answer is obvious.

We are writing our own obituaries every day that we live. Let's treasure the heritage, the legacy that is ours.

18
It Depends Upon
Your Connections

Suddenly the humdrum of calls over the squawk box of the hospital PA stopped. Instead of calling Dr. Jones or Dr. Smith, the voice over the PA system gave the emergency code, well understood by all hospital personnel. The code and the room number, then repeated again, and again.

Suddenly there was a convergence of doctors, nurses, and resuscitation personnel toward the specified room number. A patient had stopped breathing! While one doctor checked the pulse, another listened for the heart beat, and a third began compression of the chest.

Consultation was brief, knowing, thoroughly understood by those involved. Electrodes were quickly applied to the patient's chest. A sudden convulsive heaving of the chest, then a listening over the heart, and an affirmative nod of the head.

The monitor which had promptly been applied indicated that the heart had begun beating. Oxygen was administered with positive intermittent pressure. A life had been restored, literally reprieved from death.

Interestingly at this same moment a workman who unwittingly backed his heavy equipment into a high tension wire was accidentally electrocuted. The same power, the same energy, the same source. Yet one was life-giving while the other was life-taking! Ironical how nature works for us when we hold the reins, yet may turn tail and destroy us when we lose control for even a few seconds.

Satan and the Savior were both sons of the same Father. Each was a bright, intelligent spirit with more than ample promise. One chose to go his own way, resolving his own rules, doing his own thing, and taking with him all of those who preferred the same wayward way.

The other son chose to follow the proposed master plan. Because God the Father selected free agency as the sole substratum of this world, He allowed all those who so desired to follow Satan. But ever since that third part of the children of God left their Father's home, they have been wired to the wrong connection. Not only have they been electrocuted spiritually with no hope for salvation, but they have as their avowed goal to mislead as many others in the same misdirection.

In the scriptures we read that because Satan "had become miserable forever, . . . he seeketh that all men might be miserable like unto himself." (2 Nephi 2:18, 27.)

By contrast, those who follow the Savior find themselves connected to a life-sustaining, health-giving, joy-finding program. "Men are, that they might have joy," beckons the Savior.

Yes, it does depend upon how we use the power that the Lord has given us on this earth. We can connect it so that it will lead to unequivocal spiritual death; or we can harness it to free agency, connect it to the right sources, and let it lead us to eternal life.

19
Keep Temptation at Arm's Length

As a determined jogger, there are few things that keep me from it. But there are a few deterrents, such as dogs (especially those who dislike joggers), that frighten me.

Don't misunderstand. I don't dislike dogs. I just don't like them nipping at my heels, especially when their masters are not in the area to call them off.

There are joggers who carry Mace. Others carry ammonia in a squirt gun. Opposed to such methods, I had to develop my own. Although I have never really had to use it, I carry a stick, albeit a light one, that doesn't interfere with jogging.

There is something about that stick in my hand that deters dogs. It isn't even necessary to shake it at them. Somehow they know that I could use it if I had to, so they don't bother me when I carry it. And there is something about carrying that stick in my hand that makes me feel safer. As a result, the dogs and I do very well in our relationship each morning.

I wonder if there is not a lesson to be learned here.

In the mission field we always counseled our missionaries to keep an arm's length from temptation. Is it possible that the arm's length acts as a stick in the hand in many situations?

That arm doesn't have to be used against anyone.

The missionary would probably never even raise it in a gesture of self-defense. But in dealing with unsavory characters, unfit language, or dirty stories, we need to keep an arm's length away to stay out of trouble.

Nephi said: "Wilt thou make me that I may shake at the appearance of sin?" (2 Nephi 4:31.) Isn't that another way of saying: "Keep temptation at arm's length"? But the Lord doesn't do it for us. We must carry the stick. We need the courage to turn our backs and walk away when a smutty story is started by someone. We need the moral fiber to recognize and refuse inappropriate advances, whether at work, on a date, on a mission, or wherever.

This type of courage is a stick in the hand. It will not have to be used to hurt anyone, just to keep temptation and harm at arm's length.

If we will keep temptation at arm's length, we will never be handcuffed to heartaches due to sin.

20
The Key Blank

The car was locked! And the key was locked in it, and, of all inaccessible places, in the trunk! It was inconvenient. It was exasperating. It was time consuming. It was unnecessary. But I had locked the keys in the trunk of the car, and I had to pay the price.

Fortunately, when I bought the car, the keys contained tiny punched-out tabs that recorded a code for replacement of the keys should something stupid like this happen. Anticipating a situation such as this, I had carefully taped these tabs on a card and filed them away in my personal cabinet along with the title of the car.

Taking these tabs to a locksmith, I was interested to see how many different types of keys there were — all sizes, shapes, contours, and even colors. But sure enough, by following the code, he located the proper blank. By further following the directions of the code, he made a new key (several of them, for safety sake), and I was soon on my way to open the car — door and trunk.

As I pondered what had taken place in this process, I thought how very much this is like the mortal body that the Lord gives us on earth. At birth the Lord hands us a key and says: "This key will open many doors, depending upon how you shape it. It can remain as it is — a blank — thus opening no doors whatsoever. It can be 'rough hewn,' and open only a few crude locks and open those with difficulty. Or it can be carefully filed, shaped, and polished to become a master key, one that can open many doors for you."

"Choose you this day whom ye will serve," Joshua said to the children of Israel. (Joshua 24:15.) This is just about what the Lord says to us: "Take your life, do with it what you will. You have your free agency. I have given you some marvelous guidelines, but it is up to you whether you follow them or not. But if they are to take you where you want to go, the keys must fit the locks precisely."

Joshua also gave the children of Israel the code by which they could take the key blank given them by the Lord and shape for themselves a master key that would ultimately lead them back to Him. The code contained this formula: "As for me and my house, we will serve the Lord." (Joshua 24:15.)

This bit of wisdom remains a winner today. It will still unlock the doors of happiness and joy for us and for our families. And eventually this key blank can become a master key, a key that unlocks the gates for us to dwell with our families and with our Father in Heaven eternally.

21
Learn from the Leaves

It is fall. The hillsides are carpeted in a kaleidoscope of color, embossed by the contrast of towering, perenially-green pines, polka-dotted with ravishing-red maples, yolk-yellow aspen, and cloak-changing oaks. Nothing known to me can provide such a pot-pourri of splendor as the countless shades of autumn in our ageless hills. It is a feast for even the most feeble eyes.

And what provokes this majestic myriad of colors that projects nature's very own patchwork quilt on the hillsides? Would you believe — frost? How fascinating that, instead of rebelling at the nightly nipping of Jack Frost, the leaves at first smile with gentle prismatic touches here and there and finally burst into laughing hues of carmine-red, brighter than the shiniest new fire engine!

Instead of immediately folding their edges, grieving, giving up, and falling to the ground, they first turn on the most beautiful colors that nature permits them. Before they complete their life cycle they must give to the world a most majestic view of their God-given beauty in all its splendor.

Jack Frost could also teach us a lesson.

Have you ever received an icy stare from another

person for whatever reason? Have you been firmly frostbitten by a cool rejection when you have merely wanted to be friendly and helpful and warm? Wasn't your first reaction to return the same and figure they deserved it?

Have you ever been hurt, embarrassed, belittled, humiliated, cut low? If you have, it is likely that you first turned red with embarrassment, then livid with anger, and finally flushed with rage. Often our first thoughts are to return like for like, a tooth for a tooth, an eye for an eye, or even going one better for retaliation and revenge.

Such ill-tempered treatment causes unsightly scars upon our own personality which can stunt further growth and development. Occasionally we permit this ill treatment to sow seeds of hate that canker our souls and shut off the love that we normally might have for our fellowmen. Such reactions are just what the offender wanted us to have. He would like to see us act just as badly as he or she did.

It reminds us of Satan, who "seeketh that all men might be miserable like unto himself." (2 Nephi 2:27.) In other words, he is miserable, and misery loves company.

Next time try the "leaf response" to Jack Frost. Remember their response to the nipping and biting of the first blasts of cold air in the autumn. Ponder the splendor with which they responded, a splendor that splashed itself on all about it, bringing joy to all who beheld it.

A smile turns away wrath, and a joyous heart opens doors and hearts. When tempted to respond to a cold reception by bundling up and covering your face, remember the leaves and their radiant response.

22
Let Your Beacon
Light so Shine

A friend of mine is an electronic genius. His mind is constantly at work devising different ways to use electronic energy. Although his thinking is far beyond my own comprehension, I love to stand and view, even from a distance, the incredible depths of his creativity.

Especially appreciated was a tiny gadget he devised and presented to me so that I would not forget him — as if I ever could! This is a tiny solar-powered beacon light with light-sensitive cells outstretched like minuscule arms in each of the four directions feeding this energy into a mini-micro storage battery underneath the simple mechanism.

"If this unit is exposed to sunlight for just a few moments a month, it will continue to glow indefinitely," he said. And he was right. But when we moved I stored the unit in a small light-tight box for safe-keeping. It was several months before I unwrapped the package and rescued my tiny beacon light from its sunless prison.

As expected, the glow was gone. The tiny beacon functioned no longer. Even the microscopic amount of energy required had been denied, and the beacon no longer beckoned.

But as I exposed it to a few rays of sunlight the

beacon swiftly surged to life and flashed once more. It was amazing how these brief moments of light could relay their brightness to the world.

In His wisdom the Lord has counseled us "that thou mayest more fully keep thyself unspotted from the world, thou shalt go to the house of prayer and offer up thy sacraments upon my holy day." (D&C 59:9.) He knows that we need to receive some of His spiritual solar power into our souls from time to time to permit our light to shine before men and bring glory to Him.

Our participation in Church permits us an opportunity to absorb the spirit, to replenish our depleted storage batteries. It allows us to let our light (of the gospel) shine on those around us. It takes but a bit of energy to accomplish this, but if we neglect to absorb even this small amount of light, our beacon will eventually go out. And it will remain dark until its battery is recharged. We cannot be a beacon to the world when we have a dead battery.

Spiritual recharging is free to everyone. As with solar energy, God offers His goodness and power to each of us just for the taking. Let's stretch out our arms and our souls to absorb all we can so that we might give freely of this light to others.

23
Luggage Tags
Track Us Down

It was during World War II, and it was worrisome. I had to catch a plane for the West, yet I had no reservation. It was the day of discrimination, when people of higher priority "bumped" those of lower priority.

Suddenly out of almost nowhere I thought I heard someone call, "Flight Number 376 leaving Chicago for Salt Lake City." I ran to the gate to see if it was true, because I had been told there were no further planes to this destination.

The message was true, and I could see the last passenger just climbing aboard the plane. Hastening through the gate to the plane, I asked if they could squeeze in one more passenger.

"Climb aboard, soldier!" I was told. "But hurry it up. No time to wait."

I climbed aboard, realizing that I had left my only suitcase, everything I had, at the ticket counter in the airport. What would happen to my possessions and what could I wear when I arrived in Salt Lake City? I needn't have worried.

Plainly marked on the tag and securely fastened to the suitcase was my name and the address of my destination. A quick phone call from the stewardess and the suitcase was speedily on its way to the baggage room where it would board the next plane.

Perhaps the luggage could have been stolen. Possibly they could have searched for it in vain in the busy airport. There are many "ifs" in the true story that could have changed the happy ending. But in general it is true that our luggage, when properly labeled, does catch up with us.

We should be careful where we leave our label. Perhaps we should be careful to what cause or on what deed or with what words we attach our name.

Some parents feel they have nothing in worldly goods to bequeath to their children. They feel sad because they leave them no monetary inheritance.

The truth is that, whether we want to or not and whether they desire it that way or not, we do leave our children an inheritance — our reputation. Like our luggage, our record has our name stamped on it for everyone to see. And that record has a way of finding the path right back to its owner.

Is it not true that we often judge the integrity of a person by his or her family's record? "The Larsons are honest people." Or, "The Whites always pay their bills." Sometimes one might hear, "Be sure you get your money first!" Or, "Be careful of any dealings with them!"

Yes, our luggage tags do seem to track us down and leave our bags, just as we have packed them, right on our own doorsteps.

24
The Other Side of the Glass

Isn't it interesting how much one can learn from simple things in life — for instance, washing a car.

Because its color doesn't show the dirt (the color was chosen for this reason when the car was purchased), it had been quite a long time since my car had been washed. But I soon learned two things from this experience. The longer mangled bugs remain on a car, the more difficult they are to remove. The sun seems to cook them into a glue that sticks to the surface. They become part of the paint job. If the bugs can be finally removed, they leave shadowy silhouettes on the surface like those left on wallpaper by long-hung pictures.

Yes, I learned the value of frequent cleaning and careful maintenance, but the window washing taught me yet another lesson. As I cleaned the inside of the windows, the outside appeared to be dirty. When I cleaned the outside of the window, the streaks on the inside could be seen. Only the dirt on the *other* side was obvious to *my* eyes.

How like life this is. We can see the dirt, the streaks, the poor workmanship only on the other fellow's side of the glass, never on our own side. It reminds me of times I have noticed small, embarrassingly obvious pieces of food on someone else's chin, only to discover later that I had some on my own — pieces that I couldn't see until I looked into a mirror!

What a lesson in judging and prejudging!

I hope to be so busy cleaning my side of the window that I won't look at his. I hope to be so busy trying to keep the commandments myself that I'll have neither the time nor the bigotry to criticize my neighbor for *his* misbehavior.

"First cast out the beam out of thine own eye; and then shalt thou see clearly to cast out the mote out of thy brother's eye." (Matthew 7:5.)

25
The Perfect Pitch

The cacophony had continued for a nettlesome long time, as each musician independently tuned, tested, primed, and adjusted his or her instrument. Finally, to a standing ovation, the conductor made his impressive entree. All was suddenly silent.

Barely audible to the audience was a crystal-clear, perfectly pitched *A*, sounded from the pitch pipe of the conductor. By this pitch each member of the orchestra made certain his instrument was in complete harmony with the conductor's tone. Then, and only then, could the rapturous rendition begin.

True, these were master musicians, each trained both by practice and instruction to play almost to perfection. Otherwise they would never have been chosen as members of such an auspicious assemblage. Undoubtedly each had procured for himself the finest musical instrument. With endless hours of practice and under a most capable director they had now become famous for their precision and harmony.

But what if one or two had not tuned their instruments to the perfect *A* the conductor had sounded? What kind of music could they have produced, regardless of their ability to play their instruments professionally and precisely?

We have each been given a marvelous body, one that is especially adapted for us in this life. Lying dormant within that body and its mind are countless skills just waiting to be developed, trained, taught, and perfected. Using this mind and body, we are to learn how to get along with others, how to live a harmonious life.

But the Lord has also given us the privilege of constant instruction from Him. He supplies the instruction which we should follow if we desire to play to perfection. But in order to have the ultimate, masterful harmony that can come from our minds and bodies and especially from our souls, we must listen when the Lord speaks to us and make certain that our instruments (our bodies and minds) are tuned to the perfect *A* that He sounds for us.

After crying unto the Lord all day and into the night in prayer and supplication for his soul, Enos first heard a voice saying that his sins had been forgiven him. Then as he continued to pour out his soul to God, he said, "The voice of the Lord came into my mind." (Enos 10.)

When we are perfectly tuned to communicate with the Lord, we will discover that the "voice of the Lord" will come into our minds and give us the comfort and the direction that we have requested. No one needs to be spiritually tone-deaf.

Let's listen for the perfect *A* from our Master Conductor. Let's be sure we're in tune!

26
Precision Versus
Promises

We could scarcely believe our ears. Having a spouse who loves music boxes, I had heard more than my share. But this one was different. Instead of the usual "Johnny-few-notes" type of tune, the piece sounded almost like a symphony.

Turning the switch activated an amazing array of arias. Not only did it orchestrate an almost perfect pianoforte of notes, but it played three pleasurable pieces from the *Nutcracker* suite. And each note was perfectly timed and tuned.

As we stood and listened and admired, we wondered how much effort had been expended to achieve such a perfect synchronization. Perfection imposes preparation, precision, and infinite patience. The resounding result in this case was evidence that all three of these prerequisites had truly been expended.

We can learn from this masterpiece of precision. For instance, as we look at man, at his finite mind more intricate than any computer, capable of handling an estimated 14 trillion bits of information and cataloging most of it for recall, we come to the conclusion that only God in His limitless knowledge and wisdom could possibly have produced such a masterpiece.

Certainly as the Lord looks us over and admires His

handiwork He is anxious that we also perform to perfection. To insure this performance, He has given us some intelligent instructions on the care of the mind and body. He has also included a few warranties concerning these minds and bodies, carefully stating that the warranty is in force only if we follow the directions He has given us.

The Word of Wisdom was given in a time when little was known of the ill effects of smoking and drinking. Both may have been regarded as nothing more than unpleasant by both users and nonusers of the day. Little was known at that time of any health hazards to the body or mind. Now, 150 years later, medical research has vindicated the wisdom of this commandment, even to include tea and coffee.

Through our prophet the Lord has also counseled us against the use of all kinds of mind-warping drugs that deliberately derange and damage the intricate mechanisms of our mind. How can we expect masterful music to come from a mind that has been tampered with like a cheap toy?

The music box was truly a masterpiece, one that produced heavenly music. But it would not long survive a hammer or any other tool designed to disturb its carefully tuned tines. Neither will the intricate workmanship that has gone into the creation of our bodies and minds tolerate such terrible tampering.

Our bodies and minds demand the finest of care and maintenance if they are to perform with precision instead of promise.

27
Reaching Out to Reactivate

That same trail I had hiked countless times. The same moldy, cobweb-covered mines I thought I knew like the back of my hand. The same caved-in cabin lay crumbling in the curve of the canyon just where I had expected it to be.

Yet to my complete surprise I discovered on this occasion, hidden under some dense overhanging bushes, another mine. How could I have overlooked this ancient evidence of some poor old prospector's grovel for gold?

Inspecting, searching, excitedly examining this long-forgotten relic made this hike the most stimulating of the year. I couldn't help but wonder how many other camouflaged marvels we had missed as we traversed this trail over the years. This cave could so easily have been uncovered by me if I had just reached out and lifted a branch or two.

It reminded me of a friend who frequently jogs along the beach. He couldn't count the number of times he had covered that selfsame sand. Never in all his running had he unveiled anything of value. Never had it occurred to him that there might be a treasure trapped beneath his feet.

But one day he noticed a man with a metal detector scanning the same sand over which he had jogged almost daily. Every few feet this man turned up coins, jewelry, even watches and other treasures. They had been there all the time, but they had been covered by a small amount of sand.

Day after day I have passed by the homes of several of my friends who are inactive in the Church. Long ago I decided that this was their choice, that there was nothing I could do about it. *What a shame,* I thought, *that they are missing so many blessings the Church has to offer them and their lovely families. Perhaps someday they may come to see what they are missing. But right now nobody can touch them.*

Then I remembered the hike up the canyon, the cave I had missed because I had not looked closely enough. I recalled my beach-jogging friend and the treasures over which he tramped every day without knowing they were so close — if he had just looked a little deeper.

One at a time I began to look at my inactive neighbors a little deeper to see if there were some treasures about them that I had not appreciated. Were there some things I ought to know that would enhance our friendship and enable me to be a better neighbor to them?

Was it true that there was no way to uncover these precious treasures?

Is it possible that I had blindly assumed that I had "seen everything there was to see" and written these friends off, not really knowing what was in their hearts?

One by one I am discovering more about them. And the more I know, the better I like them (and I hope they like me). We are on our way to a "fellowshipping" good time together, which I hope will lead them back into the Church.

Yes, to reactivate someone, we need to reach out for him.

28
Remodeling — A Form of Repentance?

Our home was lovely when it was built. It is still lovely, comfortable, well-insulated, and secure. There are few things one could think of that it does not have. But we are remodeling it, changing it, accommodating it more to our altered type of living. And because of inflation, the cost of this remodeling closely approximates the original cost of the home.

Not only is remodeling expensive, but it is terribly inconvenient. When the home was first built we were living elsewhere and suffered no inconvenience. It didn't really matter to us how much mess the builders made, because we were not in the middle of it. Nor did it matter if it took a little longer to complete the job, because we were comfortably situated while they were doing it.

But now we are in the middle of all the dust, dirt, and debris. No matter how often we clean it up, it becomes just as dusty and dirty again the next day. It has interfered with our eating, our privacy, and even our personalities. We are so tired of the mess that we find our tempers short, our patience strained, and our communication at an all-time low.

Remodeling can be compared to life. As we build our lives, our character, our traits, our habits, how wise it is to build them well, to make any necessary alterations as we go! We should improve the product and strive for perfection in the initial plan.

How difficult it is, later in life, to effect a remodeling, a major change in the structure of our lives! Because habits become very much a part of us, it is not only inconvenient but also difficult for us to change.

Faulty ways that could have been altered so easily in youth are now firmly set, like concrete after it has dried. Only with extreme effort, infinite patience, and often with persistent pain can any improvement prevail.

Sometimes this remodeling shakes the very foundations of the body and soul. Although we know the changes will eventually produce a product well worth the price, it is terribly traumatic to tolerate at the time.

Realizing the relatively high cost of remodeling, repentance, and remorse, let's conform to the Master's plan from the beginning.

The Savior's plan requires no remodeling.

29
Satan Versus the Savior

In exasperation a father once asked his wayward son, "Just who do you think you are?" The son's response was surprising, "Dad, I wish I knew."

Who am I? has probably been the most perplexing problem man has had to solve since the beginning of time. And from the time of Adam, man has had two forces feeding him information, Satan and the Savior. Since the two forces are diametrically opposed to each other, both cannot be correct.

Satan, the master of put-downs, because he had "fallen from heaven" became miserable forever and also sought the misery of mankind. He was the originator of the phrase "Misery loves company." We read in the Book of Mormon: "For he seeketh that all men might be miserable like unto himself." (2 Nephi 2:27.)

Satan is the author of doubts, discouragement, despondency, fears and negativism. Can you imagine the Savior ever telling us that we are no good, worthless, or ever telling us to take our own lives? Certainly not. The Savior says: "Remember the worth of souls is great in the sight of God." (D&C 18:10.) "With God all things are possible." (Matthew 19:26.) "All things are possible to him that believeth." (Mark 9:23.)

Note this word of encouragement to those who might feel inadequate or unsure of themselves: "I give unto men weakness that they may be humble; and my grace is sufficient for all men that humble themselves before me; for if they humble themselves before me, and have faith in me, then will I make weak things become strong unto them." (Ether 12:27.)

Each of us is a child of God. Can you imagine a loving, understanding father not having compassion for or interest in a child and in his or her well-being?

For those of us who have qualms about our ability, those of us who are timid, hesitant, and lacking confidence in ourselves, He has given a foolproof formula. He has said: "Let virtue garnish thy thoughts unceasingly; then shall thy confidence wax strong in the presence of God." (D&C 121:45.) It's true! When we think virtuous thoughts unceasingly, all negative, downgrading, self-deprecating doubts disappear. Our confidence does return, and we begin to feel good about ourselves.

The Lord gave us some additional divine direction when He said: "And if your eye be single to my glory, your whole bodies shall be filled with light, and there shall be no darkness in you; and that body which is filled with light comprehendeth all things." (D&C 88:67.)

Can you think of a better solution to get rid of feelings of self-doubt, despair, despondency, and darkness in one's soul? When the eye is single to His glory, darkness will be replaced by light. Then we will begin to comprehend and understand ourselves and our situations; and we can successfully seek solutions for our problems and perplexities.

Jesus Christ is the Prince of Peace. He speaks peace to our hearts, to our minds, and to our souls. If the voice speaks other than peace, we know that Satan is the source.

Isn't it exciting to know that the worth of our soul is great in the sight of our Savior?

30
Sounding the Soul
for a Testimony

It was one of those times when I felt goose bumps, and that's not very often. I had been telling my friend of my feeling for the Church. Among other things I said: "I know that God lives! I know that Jesus, the Christ, is His Son. I know we have a prophet on the earth today through whom the Lord speaks and gives direction to His Church."

Right then I was challenged. "How," asked my friend, "do you know these things. You may *think* them. You may *feel* them. But you don't *know* them to be true." He thought for a minute. "Can you prove them to be true?"

Then it was my turn to think. "These things don't have to be proved to anyone," I said. "It is up to each of us to find out for himself about them — that is, if we really want to know."

"I really want to know, but I don't just want to feel. I want to *know*!"

"My friend," I said, "It is not God nor Jesus Christ nor even His Church that is on trial, but yourself." We studied each other carefully. "But the Lord has given us some guidelines to follow. First of all, though, let's dispose of this 'feeling' bit. You say you don't want to just *feel* that these things are true."

"That's right," he said.

"Do you love your wife?"

"Naturally, with all my heart."

"And I assume you love your children."

"You know better than to ask that question."

"Can you prove to me that you love them? Can you convince me how much you love them? Or is it really just something that you feel? Is it something about which there is no question? You seem so positive about it. But can you prove it to me?"

The answer was obvious.

"But I want to be able to prove to others that these beliefs are true. Can't you just take the Bible and prove them to me?" he asked.

"What I have told you is scriptural, but you'll never get what we call a witness or testimony of these things from the scriptures alone. You have to ponder, pray, perhaps fast, then start all over again. But you *can* know of a surety in your heart that they are true."

"That's what I want to know."

"Are you willing to pay the price?"

"What do you mean?"

"Are you willing to put forth the effort, the time, even the sacrifice?"

"Yes."

"Then let's start with the Book of Mormon. Turn to the third from the last page in the Book of Mormon, the tenth chapter, and read the fourth verse out loud and let's analyze it. This book carries its own promise of truthfulness that anyone can put to the test.

Together we studied it over and over and discussed each step in the promise. My friend agreed to take the test. "And isn't it unlikely that we will have genuine scripture without acknowledging that the prophets who wrote it were also genuine?" He agreed.

"There is one final test mentioned in the Bible. Let me show it to you. Let's turn to John 7:17 and read the test the Savior gave of His divinity: 'If any man will *do* his will, he shall know of the doctrine, whether it be of God, or whether I speak of myself.' "